THE LITTLE BOOK OF
VODKA

Published in 2023 by OH!
An Imprint of Welbeck Non-Fiction Limited,
part of Welbeck Publishing Group.
Offices in: London – 20 Mortimer Street, London W1T 3JW
and Sydney – 205 Commonwealth Street, Surry Hills 2010
www.welbeckpublishing.com

Compilation text © Welbeck Non-Fiction Limited 2023
Design © Welbeck Non-Fiction Limited 2023

ISBN 978-1-80069-394-4

Compiled and written by: Malcolm Croft
Editorial: Victoria Denne
Project manager: Russell Porter
Design: Tony Seddon
Production: Jess Brisley

A CIP catalogue record for this book is available from the British Library

Printed in China

10 9 8 7 6 5 4 3 2 1

THE LITTLE BOOK OF
VODKA

FILTERED
TO PERFECTION

CONTENTS

INTRODUCTION – 6

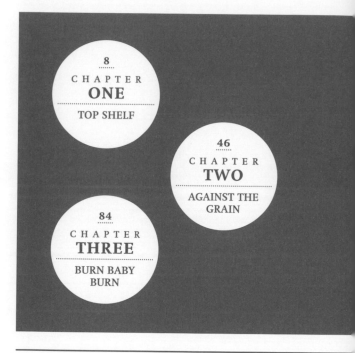

8

CHAPTER
ONE

TOP SHELF

46

CHAPTER
TWO

AGAINST THE
GRAIN

84

CHAPTER
THREE

BURN BABY
BURN

114

CHAPTER
FOUR

SHAKEN AND
STIRRED

132

CHAPTER
FIVE

LIVIN' LA VIDA
VODKA

152

CHAPTER
SIX

FIRE AND ICE

INTRODUCTION

The original bad boy of booze since the early 1950s, vodka has become the notorious weapon of choice of the super-chilled, from Tony Stark to James Bond, The Dude to Mick Jagger, Kim Kardashian to Madonna. Yes, this firestarter is set to go supernova again in the next few years if its stellar resurgence post-pandemic is anything to go by. Though, to be fair, it never really went anywhere.

For more than seven decades, vodka consistently outstripped all other spirits in sales, becoming the key ingredient in the world's most popular cocktails, and yet rarely was it elevated to the same position on pedestals as other alcoholic beverages who have, recently, found incredible fame and fortune and got a little too big for their boots. (Yeah, I'm looking at you, gin! You're just juniper-posh vodka. Remember that!)

Today, vodka is a legit top-shelf spirit that can be both sipped, shot, chased, nursed and binged, no longer the crude oil of the spirit world. Finally, spirit brands have woken to the idea that vodka, too, is worthy of "premium"-level gentrification, beloved by upmarket craft artisans, small-batch boutique vodkateers and hipster tastemakers, for the first time in its thousand-year-history. All while remaining pretty good as a carpet cleaner too, should you spill your red wine (after drinking too many vodkas).

So, let's raise a toast to this perfect drinking companion and celebrate the world's dirtiest spirit (by reputation) and its purest (by taste). With a wealth of fantastic flavours, glorious gimmicks, celebrity ambassadors and owners, and an enviable history, this tiny tome will take your tastebuds on a wild ride through stats, facts, quotes, notes, wit and tips. So, get your bottoms up, it's time to raise a toast to our fiendish friend – vodka!

Nostrovia!

CHAPTER
ONE

TOP SHELF

Since its earliest origins more than a millennia ago, vodka has been knocked back, slammed down, thrown up and kicked out more times than any sober person can count. But it always bounced back from the ropes.

Nothing can dampen the spirits of this fun-time Frankie. Where would we be without vodka? Nowhere fun, that's for sure…

The increase in worldwide sales in per cent of Ukrainian vodka, following the February 2022 Russian invasion of Ukraine. If you want to get your hand on a bottle, try Khortytsa De Luxe.

similia similibus curantur
(like cures like)

The Latin precursor to
"Hair of the dog" that dates
to the time of Hippocrates,
2,500 years ago.

"

Take a shot of
vodka and hope
for the best.

"

Nathan Lane

❝

I no longer know
if I wish to drown
myself in love,
vodka or the sea.

❞

Franz Kafka

2

The number of kilograms of wheat to make a bottle of 750ml vodka. That's about the same weight as a human brain, or four 1 lb bags of sugar.

110

The amount, in billions of litres, of ethanol produced globally in 2021. Sugar cane and corn are the main feedstocks.

The best thing about vodka is that you don't have to wait ages for it to mature in barrels or bottles. It's best enjoyed immediately!

66

I believe that if life
gives you lemons,
you should make
lemonade... And try to
find somebody whose
life has given them
vodka and have a party.

99

Ron White

"

There's no absolutes in life – only vodka.

"

Mick Jagger

Gin is nothing
more than vodka
infused with
juniper berries.

In Ukraine,
vodka is always
traditionally sold
at a bar with
a pickle.

The 2022 World Vodka Awards, part of the World Drinks Awards, crowned New Zealand's Broken Heart Vodka as the "World's Best Pure and Neutral Vodka".

Broken Heart is made with the finest spring water from Arrowtown, New Zealand and is "delectably pure and clean with soft notes of lemon".

As you well know, vodka is colourless. But it doesn't have to be. Add food colouring – any colour you like! – to your next shot.

That'll brighten up the burn.

> I have a punishing
> workout regimen.
> Every day I do three
> minutes on a treadmill,
> then I lie down, drink
> a glass of vodka, and
> smoke a cigarette.

Anthony Hopkins

"

If wine is fruit, then vodka must be a vegetable.

"

Jann Arden

Long considered the purest
of all spirits, vodka is made
from just two ingredients:
60 per cent ethanol
and
40 per cent water.
The ethanol is produced by
fermenting a base ingredient
that turns starch into sugar.
In vodka, most commonly,
these are: wheat, rye, corn,
and potato.

Unlike red wine, or whisky, if you spill a glass of vodka, you don't have to clean up the mess.*

As well as an intoxicating spirit, vodka doubles as a decent disinfectant (and antibacterial agent) that can dissolve dirt and grease – especially if it was a double serving. So, if you spill it, leave it. It'll clean itself up eventually, right?

*Sadly, vodka doesn't polish your insides clean.

Hollywood actor Channing Tatum's small-batch vodka brand, Born and Bred, is using Idaho Potatoes and glacial water from the Teton Mountains, Idaho. It is distilled 20 times to create a smooth, clean vodka. "I'm a stripper that became an actor that now works in vodka.

"Nothing surprises me anymore," he said.

"

Vodka is kind of a hobby.

"

Betty White

66

Money, like vodka, turns a person into an eccentric.

99

Anton Chekhov

"

Vodka eyeballing sounds great, but it's a slippery slope.
Next, you'll be scotch nostriling, tequila nippling and, before you know it, Jager tainting.

"

Stephen Colbert

In 2010, "Vodka eyeballing" became a social media phenomenon. It is the practice of imbibing a vodka shot... through the eye sockets. Followers of this "chilly willy" fashion, as it is known in slang, believed vodka was absorbed into the bloodstream faster through the mucous membranes of the eyeball.

Does it work? No.

Lucille Bluth:
"Get me a vodka rocks."

Michael Bluth:
"Mom, it's breakfast."

Lucille Bluth:
"And a piece of toast."

Lucille Bluth, Arrested Development

66

Shaken, not stirred, will get
you cold water with a dash
of [vodka] and dry vermouth.
The reason you stir it with
a special spoon is so not to
chip the ice. James [Bond] is
ordering a weak martini and
being snooty about it.

99

President Bartlet, The West Wing

66

Vodka is tasteless going down, but it is memorable coming up.

99

Garrison Keillor

> **"**
> # Wine we need for health, and the health we need to drink vodka.
> **"**

Viktor Chernomyrdin

Vodka Martini

Serving Suggestion
- 1 tbsp dry vermouth
- 60 ml vodka
- Olive, or lemon peel, to garnish

Make It Right
Drown the dry vermouth with the vodka.
Throw in some ice and shake together in
a cocktail shaker to combine. Strain into a
chilled martini glass. Dunk an olive, or a twist
of lemon peel.

66

Two vodka martinis,
extra dry, extra olives,
extra fast. Make one of
them dirty, will you?

99

Tony Stark, Iron Man, 2008

9

The number of White Russians
The Dude (Jeff Bridges) drinks in Coen
Brothers cult classic *The Big Lebowski*.
His homemade recipe is simple: two
parts vodka, one part Kahlua, one part
cream. During the film, The Dude calls
his drink a "Caucasian".

Hey, careful, man,
there's a beverage here!

The Dude

"
Vodka. That's what
they [Russians]
drink, isn't it?
Never water.
"

Jack D. Ripper, Dr. Strangelove

66

Apparently vodka helps
flowers last longer
when they're dying.
But you can put vodka
in anything, and it'll
make it better.

99

Drew Barrymore

66

We drank our coffee
the Russian way. That
is to say we had vodka
before it and vodka
afterwards.

Philip Sington

100

The number of calories,
per 50 ml double
measure, in vodka.
Vodka is considered
the least calorific spirit
on the top shelf.
It has zero carbs.

Contrary to popular myth, an open bottle of vodka doesn't last forever, especially if not stored properly. Light, temperature and air all change the way vodka tastes.

It's recommended to keep open bottles of vodka in the fridge for no longer than two years.

Vodka must be
80 per cent proof
– 40 per cent ABV
(when mixed with
60 per cent water).

Anything less – or more
– just isn't vodka.

In 1985, four members of a Soviet tank crew became lost during manoeuvres when darkness fell in cold, wet and foggy weather in Czechoslovakia. Thirsty, they swapped their tank for 24 bottles of vodka with a local bar owner, who also threw in some herring and pickles "as a gesture of comradeship".

The soldiers were found in a forest two days later, sleeping off the booze. News of the story was only discovered when the owner of a local metal-recycling centre reported to the military that a "large amount of high-quality, sawed-up steel" had been dropped off from the pub owner. Ironically, the soldiers had only ran out of vodka because rations had been cut as part of a Soviet government campaign against alcoholism.

CHAPTER
TWO

AGAINST THE GRAIN

Vodka is a rule-breaker. It's devoid of form, taste and colour, and yet, there are hundreds of global vodka brands that tell us their own tasty stories. It burns like Hell even when it's ice cold. It's smooth, even when a grainy variety. It's a chaser, but also a leader. It's the perfect mixer, blending in wherever it goes, yet it's the firestarter other spirits rely on.

Come sit, and sip, with us as we go against the grain…

Following the Russian invasion of Ukraine in 2022, premium vodka brand Vodka 4 Peace launched Vodka Zelensky, named after the Ukrainian president and hero. 100 per cent of profits will go to assist Ukraine's fightback.

66

I began to think vodka was my drink at last. It didn't taste like anything, but it went straight down into my stomach like a sword swallowers' sword and made me feel powerful and godlike.

99

Sylvia Plath, The Bell Jar

"

I blew the lot on vodka and tonic, gambling and fags. Looking back, I think I overdid it on the tonic.

"

Stan Bowles

"

I love vodka martinis. I know it's a cliché.

"

Daniel Craig

Bond on Vodka:
Part 1

When it comes to vodka, Bond said a little more than just "shaken, not stirred".

"Three measures of Gordon's, one of vodka, half a measure of Kina Lillet. Shake it very well until it's ice-cold, then add a large thin slice of lemon peel. Got it?"

James Bond's "Vesper" Martini, as described in Casino Royale, *2006*

"Russian vodka. Well done."

You Only Live Twice, *1967*

"Vodka, rather shaken, and one microchip."

A View to a Kill, *1985*

"Vodka martini, plenty of ice…
if you can spare it."
Die Another Day, 2002

"Mr. Bond will have Vodka martini,
shaken, not stirred."
Tomorrow Never Dies, 1997

"Oh, please, James, spare me the Freud. I
might as well ask you for the vodka martinis
that have silenced the screams of all the men
you've killed… or if you find forgiveness in the
arms of all those willing women, for all the
dead ones you failed to protect."
Goldeneye, 1995

"A medium Vodka Dry Martini – with a slice of
lemon peel. Shaken and not stirred please. I
would prefer Russian or Polish vodka."
Dr No, 1952

Top Ten Bestselling Vodkas 2021

Per million bottles:
1. Smirnoff – *318*
2. Absolut – *140*
3. Khortytsa – *130*
4. Żubrówka – *129*
5. Morosha – *95*
6. Nemiroff – *67*
7. Soplica – *55*
8. Grey Goose – *47*
9. Magic Moments – *44*
10. Ketel One – *40*

That's more than one billion bottles in total!

"

Who wants an orange whip? Orange whip?
Orange whip? Three orange whips!

"

In the seminal movie, *The Blues Brothers*, John
Candy's character, Detective Burton Mercer,
orders this little-known cocktail, the Orange
Whip. The cocktail was not mentioned in
the original script. However, Kenny Dugan,
Orange Whip's sales director at the time,
was providing refreshments for the cast and
asked if his product could be mentioned in the
film. Director John Landis spoke about this to
Candy, who improvised the line. Following the
film's success, the cocktail experienced a huge
resurgence in popularity.

Just blend a shot each of rum, vodka, cream
and orange juice into a frothy milkshake and
then pour over ice in a tall glass.

"

Rock stars exercising? I don't think it's right. I drink too much but you won't catch me doing sit-ups or jogging. You see pictures of Bono running around LA with his little white legs and a bottle of Volvic and he looks like a fanny. I mean, maybe if it was a bottle of vodka.

"

Liam Gallagher

56

Next time you're in the
shower, give your hair
a shot of vodka after
conditioning – it will
give it an extra shine by
lowering your hair's pH.

Donald Trump's vodka brand, Trump Vodka, was an absolute disaster. "By the summer of '06, I fully expect the most called-for cocktail in America to be the 'T&T' or the 'Trump and tonic,'" Trump said. "It's a smooth vodka, it's a great-tasting vodka – very high level, very high style," he said, despite being a non-drinker.

Despite its slogan – "Success Distilled" – Trump Vodka was discontinued in 2011.

Leo Tolstoy, Russian author of *War and Peace*, and regarded as one of the greatest writers of all time, loathed his nation's dependence on vodka. To combat its destruction, Tolstoy founded a temperance society called "Union Against Drunkenness". They went round sticking a skull and crossbones "Poison" label on vodka bottles.

October 4

is National Vodka Day.
How will you celebrate?

Electric Hendrix Vodka

In 2009, the makers of a vodka named after 1960s rock legend, Jimi Hendrix, were ordered by a federal judge in the U.S. to pay $3.2 million in damages for infringing on trademarks and licensing rights owned by the late guitarist's estate. Janie Hendrix, Jimi's stepsister, said that using Jimi's image to sell alcohol was a "sick joke". Odd choice of words, considering Jimi Hendrix died from choking on his own vomit, after drinking too much alcohol, in 1970.

The Cosmopolitan cocktail was made iconic by the 1990s TV show, *Sex and the City*. However, its origins were a little less sexy. It started off as a health gimmick started by the juice brand Ocean Spray in 1968. The brand wanted to market cranberry juice to adults, so launched a marketing campaign around a vodka-cranberry-lime cocktail they called the Harpoon. It was in 1987 that it became the Cosmopolitan, with the addition of triple sec, a move credited to a Manhattan bartender. A few years later, Carrie Bradshaw and her gal-pals made the cocktail famous when it became their favourite.

In the first *SATC* movie, the girls even made a joke out OF THE drink's popularity from their influence. "Why did we ever stop drinking these?" Charlotte asked. To which Carrie replied, "Because everyone else started."

Vodka Playlist: Songs that Feel the Burn

1. "Burning Love" – Elvis Presley
2. "Fire Water Burn" – Bloodhound Gang
3. "Burning For You" – Blue Oyster Cult
4. "Burn it Down" – Linkin Park
5. "Burning Desire" – Lana Del Ray
6. "Burn" – Deep Purple
7. "Something's Burning" – Kenny Rogers
8. "Burn Baby Burn" – Ash
9. "Burning Down the House" – Talking Heads
10. "Slow Burn" – David Bowie

66

Vodka is a very deceptive drink, because you drink it and you think, 'What is this? This is pointless! You can't taste it; you can't smell it... Why did we waste our money on this – bloody hell, why are we on a traffic island?'

99

Dylan Moran

"
I think that's what
I love about the vodka,
is that it's consistent.
It's consistent in its
pureness.
"

Robert De Niro

❝

I'd like a cheeseburger,
please, large fries, and
a Cosmopolitan!

❞

Carrie Bradshaw, Sex and the City

"

Start drinking vodka instead of beer and try to get a six-pack as early as possible and you'll be a much more successful actor.

"

Robert Pattinson

Choose Your Base

Vodka's fermentable base ingredient can be literally anything that converts starch into sugars. Most vodka is either rye, wheat, or corn grain. What is your favourite vodka made of?

Barley
Finlandia

Corn
Crystal Head
Deep Eddy
Prairie Organic
Smirnoff

Grape
Cîroc
Pears
St. George

Rye
Belvedere
Sobieski
Square One
Sweet Potato
Corbin

Potato
Blue Ice
Chopin
Christiania
Grand Teton
Luksusowa
Vikingfjord

Whey
VDKA 6100
Black Cow

Wheat
42 Below
Absolut
Grey Goose
Ketel One
Leaf
Pinnacle
Russian Standard
Svedka
Three Olives
Stolichnaya
(wheat and rye)

52

The amount of ethanol, in billions of litres, the U.S. produced in 2020 – half of the entire world's supply.

66

It'll take you a
couple of vodka and
tonics to set you on
your feet again.

99

Elton John

Voiceless velar plosive

In phonetics, this is the name given to the consonant sound of the hard K in vodka.

Hair of the Dog

As the lightest and purest spirit, it is commonly accepted that vodka is both the best booze to drink to get drunk with the least amount of hangover as well as the best booze to drink to cure a hangover.

The expression "hair of the dog" originates from the turn of the nineteenth century and prescribes a method of treatment for a rabid dog bite. By placing hair from the dog in the bite wound, the bitten victim won't endure "evil consequences".

"

Russian vodka is OK if you need to clean the oven. For drinking, it must henceforth be Polish.

"

Hugh Laurie

66

I spilled some vodka
on the carpet, and I
vacuumed it up, and
the vacuum got drunk.
I had to take the
Hoover to detox.

99

Mitch Hedberg

Top 5: Vodka in the UK

Bottles bought in 2021:
1. Smirnoff Red – *6,330,660*
2. Absolut Blue – *531,516*
3. Ketel One – *330,144*
4. Grey Goose – *286,260*
5. Absolut Vanilla – *273,924*

Pornstar Martini

Serving Suggestion
- 25 ml vanilla-infused vodka
- 25 ml Passoã
- 25 ml passionfruit puree
- 25 ml apple juice
- 2 tsp vanilla sugar
- 35 ml champagne
- Half a passion fruit shell

Make It Right
Mix the vodka, Passoã, passionfruit puree, apple juice and vanilla sugar into a cocktail shaker with ice. Shake. Strain into a chilled cocktail glass, and top with the fizz. Garnish with the passionfruit shell.

"

Most important, the U.S. should be candid with Russia when our views do not coincide. We are great world powers, and our interests will inevitably clash, but the greatest mistake we can make is to try to drown down differences in vodka toasts at 'feel-good' summit meetings.

"

Richard Nixon, before his death in 1994

66

I'm drinking
my milk.

99

Roger Sterling*, Mad Men

*Roger's infamous work drink of choice was a glass of milk, one ice cube, with vodka loaded on top. He rarely bothered to stir.

"

Different vodkas have different effects. Some make you feel a little… poly-lingual. Some make you feel like you want to talk back to someone who's giving you a hard time. Some make you feel like lifting kettle bells.

"

Bill Murray

In November 2022, Daniel Craig became the newest brand ambassador for Belvedere Vodka, James Bond's vodka tipple in 2015's *Spectre*. To celebrate, he teamed up with director Taika Waititi to shoot a cinematic two-minute commercial. Starring "as himself", Craig suggestively gyrates, free of all inhibition, from Paris' Pont Neuf to the prestigious Cheval Blanc Hotel. He then spins the bottle in a lobby, before splashing in the pool and cutting some serious rug on the rooftop bathed in lights. Eventually Craig sits in his room and takes a sip of vodka, exclaiming "Finally", before Waititi demands "Let's go again, just be yourself!" Craig then flashes us a knowing smile, showing off diamond-encrusted monogrammed teeth, before his voiceover purrs, "Belvedere Vodka…*mmmmmm*."

Yes, it really is as bonkers as it sounds.

66

The three-martini
lunch is the epitome
of American efficiency.
Where else can you get
an earful, a bellyful,
and a snootful at the
same time?

99

Gerald Ford

13

The value, in Scrabble points, of the word "vodka".

CHAPTER
THREE

BURN BABY BURN

Around the world, vodka is known under many nicknames. From "burn wine" to "potato juice", to the iconic "voddy". Yep, this firewater breathes flames into your glass, filling it with history, flavour and memories all at the same time. Let's light the fuse and let this booze be our muse… away we go!

The best-selling spirit in the U.S. throughout the COVID-19 pandemic was Tito's Vodka. On average it sold a bottle every five minutes.

Here's the Top Ten:
1. Tito's Homemade – Vodka
   (124 million bottles in 2020!)
2. Casamigos – Tequila
3. Bulleit – Bourbon
4. Jameson – Whiskey
5. Jack Daniels – Whiskey
6. Espolón – Tequila
7. Don Julio – Tequila
8. Patron – Tequila
9. Johnnie Walker – Whisky
10. Smirnoff – Vodka

Mr Beverage

The founder of Tito's Homemade Vodka, one of the most successful independent vodka brands of all time, is Bert Beveridge. Beveridge started the company in 1997 using $90,000 borrowed across 19 credit cards. In 2001, Tito's was crowned best vodka at the World Spirits Competition in San Francisco, beating 72 vodka brands.

"It's just real good vodka," Beveridge says. "The cleanest and purest spirit ever tested!"

In 2016, the UK's Andi Doherty downed an entire litre of vodka in eight seconds in a bid to break the "world's stupidest record" and prove he could "drink the most vodka in the world".

"I'm fully up for doing it in front of Guinness World Record officials to become the verified champion," he said. Guinness World Records declined to record the stunt due to it being "reckless" and "life-threatening".

"

Vodka is like
water, but with
consequences.

"

Tom Rachman

"

He knows just how I like my martini – full of alcohol.

"

Homer Simpson

The famous "Big Boy Milkshake" – a White Russian – is a vodka cocktail known by many names. It's also called a White Canadian (with goat's milk), a Blind Russian (with Bailey's ice cream), a White Cuban (with rum instead of vodka), and, hilariously, an Anna Kournikova (with low-fat milk, instead of cream).

Vodka historians aren't entirely sure where the spirit first flowed. What is known is that it was either Poland, in the 700s, or Russia, a century later. Russians called it "voda"; Polish called it "woda".

The origin of the word, though disputed, is believed to come from the Polish "Gorzałka" (gore-zaw-ka), derived from "gorzeć" – Polish for "to burn".

When it comes to numbers of distillations, a wheat/rye/corn vodka only needs to be twice or triple distilled. Any more is just marketing.

For potato vodka, more distillations are acceptable due to a higher level of impurities.

100 grams

In August 1941, during World War II, Joseph Stalin officially decreed that frontline Soviet soldiers were to be issued two daily cups (100 grams) of vodka. It was called "the Commissar's Ration". The vodka was to combat nerves, exhaustion and the cold, and also to act as a morale booster.

1:10 a.m., May 9, 1945

A radio report echoed around Russia that Nazi Germany had officially surrendered to the Soviet Union. The war was over. Russians immediately took to the streets to celebrate.

A day later, when Stalin addressed the nation, that nation had drunk all the vodka! "On May 10, it was impossible to buy vodka in Moscow, because it was completely drunk," reported naval navigator Nikolai Kryuchkov.

3,750,000

The price, in dollars, of a single bottle of Billionaire Vodka, officially the world's most expensive vodka.

The vodka is first ice-filtered, then filtered through Nordic birch charcoal, and then, finally, passed through sand made from crushed diamonds and gems.

It is bottled in a platinum- and rhodium-encased, diamond-encrusted crystal bottle.

Before going almost teetotal, Keith, guitarist for the Rolling Stones, loved vodka. His favourite cocktail was called Nuclear Waste – vodka drenched with orange, cranberry juice and Fanta.

A Toast... to Toasts!

Like most nations who like to drink, toasts are an important, and often complex, social ritual. Here's ten traditional toasts to twist your tongue around!

Na zdrowie! – To health!

Sto lat! – One hundred years!

Człowiek nie wielbłąd, pić musi! – Man is not a camel, he must drink!

Rybka lubi popływać! – Fish like to swim!

Za nas! – To us!

Za piękne panie! – For beautiful women!

Zdrowie pięknych pań oraz mojej żony! –
To the health of the beautiful ladies…
and my wife!

Na drugą nogę! – For the second leg!

Chluśniem bo uśniem! – Here's mud
in your eye!

Za tych co nie mogą! – For those who
cannot drink!

50 grams

Vodka weighs less than water. One litre of Vodka weighs 50 grams lighter than one litre of water.

Say that five times fast.

Screwdriver

Truman Capote called his favourite cocktail, the Screwdriver, "my orange drink". Now it's all yours…

Serving Suggestion
- 1 large or 2 small oranges
- 1 clementine
- 2 large ice cubes
- 50 ml vodka
- Splashes of Angostura bitters
- Orange wedge

Make It Right
Squeeze the juice from the oranges and clementine into a glass filled with two large ice cubes. Drown with the vodka. Stir. Then add the Angostura bitters and the orange wedge. Done!

September 28, *1914*

Tsar Nicholas II, whose government had a monopoly over all vodka production, proclaimed, "I have already decided to abolish forever the government sale of vodka in Russia." He wanted his people, and recruitments to the Army, to remain sober during World War I.

The famed mystic, Rasputin, agreed. "It is unbefitting for a Tsar to deal in vodka and make drunkards out of honest people. The time has come to lock up the Tsar's saloons."

The peasants, and soldiers, disagreed, claiming, "Never since the dawn of human history had a single country, in a time of war, renounced the principal source of its revenue."

At the time, one third of all government revenue came from vodka sales.

66

The three most
astonishing things in
the past half-century
were The Blues, Cubism,
and Polish Vodka.

Pablo Picasso

Bloody Mary

Invented in the 1930s, in New York, the
Bloody Mary has become a worldwide staple
for weekend brunches – and the ideal
Hair of the Dog.

Serving Suggestion
- Two large ice cubes
- 100 ml vodka
- 500 ml tomato juice
- 1 tbsp lemon juice, plus 2 slices to serve
- 3 drops of Worcestershire sauce
- 3 drops of Tabasco
- Pinch celery salt
- Pinch black pepper
- 2 celery sticks, to serve

Make It Right
Soak the ice in the vodka, tomato juice and lemon juice. Add your desired drops of Worcestershire sauce and Tabasco and a pinch of celery salt and pepper. Stir and strain and serve. Dunk a celery stick or two.

1934

The year the first Smirnoff
vodka plant opened for
business (and pleasure) in
Bethel, Connecticut, USA.

66

The phone rings, and a voice on the other end says, 'How would you like to be this year's vodka man?' And I said 'No. I'm an artist, I do not do commercials. I don't pander. I don't drink vodka. And if I did I wouldn't drink your product.' And he said, 'Too bad, it pays fifty thousand dollars.' And I said, 'Hold on. I'll put Mr Allen on the phone.'

99

Woody Allen (one of the first U.S. celebrities to advertise vodka – Smirnoff – in the 1960s)

1546

Unlike Russian Tsar Ivan the Terrible's monopoly on vodka production, In 1546, Poland's King Jan Olbracht allowed all Polish citizens to legally make and sell vodka. It led to an explosion of family-made vodkas, each offering something different.

Pyotr Smirnov, the creator of Smirnoff, was a peasant who built an empire out of vodka, creating the world's best-selling vodka. When he died in 1898, he was worth $130 million and was one of the richest men in Russia.

That's around $20 billion today.

Pyotr's son, Vladimir, fled to France after the Bolshevik revolution and took his father's recipe with him. "Smirnoff" is the French spelling of his name.

In 2022, a TikTok trend revealed that pouring cheap vodka through a water filter makes the vodka taste like a premium vodka. The water filter, with its activated carbon filter, cuts out the chlorine taste and odour (the strong smell you can feel in the back of your nostrils when drinking bottom-shelf vodka) and filters out more impurities, making the vodka cleaner, smoother and purer.

Do try this at home!

The Vodka Belt

The world's significant producers and consumers of vodka are part of what is known as the Vodka Belt. Your mission, should you choose to accept it, is to try vodka from each one. Off you go:

1. Sweden
2. Norway
3. Iceland
4. Finland
5. Estonia
6. Latvia
7. Lithuania
8. Russia
9. Belarus
10. Ukraine
11. Poland
12. Slovakia

The percentage of vodka that is imported from Russia to America. Most vodka enjoyed in the U.S. is made … in the U.S.

According to Statista, in 2022, the worldwide vodka market was valued at

41.63 billion

U.S. dollars. By 2025, it is forecasted to reach a value of 58 billion dollars, with a 10 per cent growth each year.

CHAPTER
FOUR

SHAKEN AND STIRRED

For 70 years, James Bond's weapon of choice at the bar has always been vodka, drinking more than 19 vodka martinis throughout his literary origins, and 21 across the 25 blockbuster films. That's a lot of vodka! But while Bond may be responsible for shooting this spirit directly into our brains, he isn't the only champion of it. Many more icons have imbibed this fine spirit, and lived to tell the tale…

Top Ten: Vodka Brands Owned by Celebrities

1. Crystal Skull – Dan Ackroyd
2. Slovenia Vodka – Bill Murray
3. Bedlam Vodka – Jason Derulo
4. Chopin Vodka – Vera Wang
5. CÎROC – Sean "Diddy" Combs
6. VDKA 6100 – Robert De Niro
7. Born and Bred American Craft Vodka – Channing Tatum
8. King St. Vodka – Kate Hudson
9. Smithworks American Made Vodka – Blake Shelton
10. Voli 305 Vodka – Pitbull
11. TRUE Vodka – Mike Piazza

90 per cent

of the vodka
Russians drink
is Russian.

Hollywood actor,
and legendary
boozehound, Richard
Burton considered
himself sober when he
only drank one bottle
of vodka a day.

Vodka accounts for
23 per cent
of all spirit sales in
the world.

CH_3CH_2OH

The chemical formula
of ethanol.

All you need to make vodka
is a little H_2O.

After distillation and
filtration, a vodka's alcohol
percentage will reach

96 per cent.

A dilution of 40 per cent
water will turn the liquid
into commercial, and
legal, vodka.

Vodka Consumption by Nation

Shots per month per person:

1. Russia – *17.28*
2. Poland – *13.71*
3. Ukraine – *9.96*
4. Bulgaria – *5.26*
5. Slovakia – *4.13*
6. United States of America – *3.76*
7. Ireland – *3.38*
8. Finland – *3.19*
9. United Kingdom – *3.01*
10. Hungary – *2.63*

The first 35 per cent of a vodka distillation results in an ethanol that is highly toxic and is thrown away. This is called the "heads".

The next 30 per cent of the distillation is the best and is called the "hearts". This is what is put into bottles.

The final 35 per cent, the "tails", is distilled further.

When choosing the nation's religion, Vladimir the Great, the ruler of Russia from 980 to 1015, reportedly chose Christianity over Islam because Christianity allowed him to drink.

"Drinking is the joy of Russia. We cannot do without it!" he proclaimed.

1941

The legendary Moscow Mule was invented one night at the Chatham Hotel, New York, when John Morgan, owner of a failing ginger beer company, and John Martin, owner of Smirnoff, met to discuss their inability to sell their products.

In a stroke of genius, the two decided to mix business with pleasure and poured the ginger beer and Smirnoff together with ice and a squeeze of lemon juice. The Moscow Mule was born! So called because the ginger beer gives the vodka a little kick!

Cosmopolitan

Serving Suggestion
- 45 ml lemon vodka
- 15 ml triple sec
- 30 ml cranberry juice
- 10 ml lime juice
- Ice
- Orange zest, or a lime wedge on the rim of the glass.

Make It Right
Shake vodka, triple sec, cranberry juice and lime juice together with the ice. Strain into a cocktail glass. With a match, light the orange zest, so that orange oils are released, then drop it into your drink.

"

To be honest, I really do love a Cosmopolitan. Strangely enough, it didn't happen until long after I stopped shooting *Sex and the City* and the movies. I would be served them at restaurants, or people sent them over. But I didn't really drink the cocktail until after we finished the show. I went to some place and had an exquisite one and then it started.

"

Sarah Jessica Parker

1405

The first written recording of the word "wódka" appeared in Poland in 1405, in court documents from the Sandomierz Court Registry. It related to medicine and cosmetic cleaners, a large usage of vodka (ethanol and water) at the time.

In 2021, Americans spent
$7.3 billion
on vodka – more than any
other spirit. One in three
bottles ordered in bars
were vodka.

In June 1950, at the height of the Cold War, U.S. bartenders went on strike. They paraded down Fifth Avenue to protest Russian Vodka, pouring it down drains, believing the profits of its sale went to undermine U.S. democracy. They carried a banner that read, "Down with the Moscow Mule – We Don't Need Smirnoff Vodka!" It had the opposite effect.

Smirnoff's then-owner, John Martin, announced, "It was great. All the people who saw the sign were rushing into the bars to try the drink."

> **“**
> Vodka is neutral spirits so distilled, or so treated after distillation with charcoal or other materials, as to be without distinctive character, aroma, taste or colour.
> **”**

Alcohol and Tobacco Tax and Trade Bureau, 1962*

* In 2021, this definition was changed to "A neutral spirit which may be treated with up to 2 grams per litre of sugar and up to 1 gram per litre of citric acid" and removed the qualifier "without distinctive taste.".

This change signalled, for the first time in 60 years, that it was legally permissible for vodka to taste differently.

CHAPTER
FIVE

LIVIN' LA VIDA VODKA

From Russian Tsars to rock 'n' roll
stars, celebs to plebs, mules to fuels,
and presidents to princesses,
vodka is enjoyed by just about
everything and everyone.

It's great to drink with, clean your
teeth with, and drive cars with. You
can't say that about red wine, can you?
Let's take a closer look…

66

Death is preferable to selling vodka!

99

Vladimir Lenin

In 1917, as part of the Russian Revolution, Premier Vladimir Lenin banned the sale of vodka, making Russia the first nation on earth to suffer prohibition. He said, "We should not follow the example of the capitalist countries and put vodka and other intoxicants on the market, because, profitable though they are, they will lead us back to capitalism and not forward to communism."

In 1924, after Lenin's death, his successor, Joseph Stalin, got the nation drinking again, believing that prohibition was tantamount to economic sabotage. Between 1955 and 1979, vodka consumption doubled.

25

The percentage of Russian men who die before the age of 55 due predominantly to liver cirrhosis.* In the UK, that figure is 7 per cent. Russian adults drink 20 litres of vodka per year. The average Briton drinks about three litres of spirits.

*The World Health Organization has recently revealed that in the past decade, Russian alcohol consumption has decreased by 43 per cent.

Lemon Drop

Serving Suggestion
- 60 ml vodka
- Lemon juice (3 squeezed lemons should suffice)
- 2 tbsp sugar
- 3 fresh mint leaves

Make It Right
Shake the vodka, lemon juice, and sugar in a cocktail shaker. Strain into a sugar-rimmed martini glass. Garnish with mint. Let the sweet times roll…

Drink Vodka Like a Russian

Russian vodka drinking etiquette is infamously complicated. There are rules to obey!

1. The first shot must be immediately followed by the second!
2. Toast every shot. Never fill just your own glass. The person pronouncing the toasts is responsible for filling everyone's glasses.
3. Each toast for each shot must be different.
4. Pure vodka only. No mixers. And it must be served supremely cold – and drank fast.
5. If you turn up late to the party, you must neck a "penalty shot".
6. As soon as a bottle is empty, hide it. Russians don't like empty bottles kept on tables – it's a bad omen!

7. Never say no to the final shot – the "na
   pososhok" (the lucky shot) of the night.
   It's rude.
7. You can only skip a shot before the vodka
   is poured.
8. "Washing the purchase" is a custom in
   many countries. Bought a new house or car?
   You celebrate with your neighbour with
   vodka. According to legend, this is to stop
   your neighbour from becoming jealous.
9. A party of drinkers should never be less
   than three people. A popular phrase in
   Russia, "Soobrazitnatroikh" means "think
   for three". This phrase is used when two
   people require a third one to join them
   for drinks.
10. Before the end of the night, offer your
    guests ten shots, one for each step toward
    the door.

Mick Jagger, frontman of
the Rolling Stones, is perhaps
the most famous vodka
rock 'n' roller. In the 1970s,
he became known for his love
of vodka mixed with orange
and pineapple juice. He
also used to make breakfast
pancakes with vodka too.

Moscow Mule

Serving Suggestion
- Crushed ice
- 50 ml vodka
- 150–200 ml ginger beer
- A few splashes of ginger bitters
- 1 wedge of lime
- 1 sprig of mint

Make It Right
Load a glass with crushed ice, then drench in vodka. Fill to the top with the ginger beer and stir. Add a dash or two of ginger bitters. Squeeze the lime and dunk the mint.

"

Never forget the rule for Mule – make it with Smirnoff.

"

Smirnoff print ad, 1966.

Vodka didn't appear in bars, or liquor stores, in the U.S. until after the repeal of prohibition in 1933. It soon overtook gin as the No.1 consumed liquor. Why? Because it could be mixed with anything – and Americans were desperate for a drink!

318,000,000

Smirnoff vodka was the leading global vodka brand in 2021, selling 26.5 million 9-litre cases, or 318 million bottles. That's one-third of all vodka sold worldwide each year.

In 2022, the UK vodka industry is worth

£3 billion,

approximately one-third of the overall UK spirit market.

Sweden

The world's largest vodka exporter in 2021, selling almost half-a-billion dollars' worth. France came second.

In 2020, 4 out of 10 of America's bestselling spirits were vodka.

1. Tito's Handmade – Vodka
2. Smirnoff – Vodka
3. Crown Royal Canadian – Whiskey
4. Bacardi – Rum
5. Jim Beam Family – Whiskey
6. Fireball – Cordials and Liqueurs
7. New Amsterdam – Vodka
8. Captain Morgan – Rum
9. Jack Daniels – Whiskey
10. Svedka – Vodka

1976

The year that vodka surpassed whiskey as the U.S.'s best-selling spirit for the first time. It has been the top-selling spirit in the States since then.

It was John G. Martin who, in 1939, bought the U.S. rights to sell Smirnoff for a measly $14,000. "I'll never know why," he said, "The decision was based on pure instinct."

Martin marketed the spirit as "White whiskey — no colour, no smell, no taste."

It worked.

The world's largest importers of vodka:

1. USA – *51 per cent* ($1.37 billion)
2. United Kingdom – *4.64 per cent* ($124 million)
3. Canada – *4.6 per cent* ($123 million)
4. Germany – *4.11 per cent* ($110 million)
5. France – *3.63 per cent* ($97 million)
6. Italy – *1.95 per cent* ($52 million)

> **The truth was, vodka was my only ally.**

Carrie Bradshaw, Sex and the City

CHAPTER
SIX

FIRE AND ICE

Welcome to your sixth shot of vodka-related trivia. Congratulations on making it this far. Hopefully, your eyesight is still functioning. We're not slr.. slrir… slurb… slurring our words, just yet.

It's time to raise a toast to this exquisite spirit before bed beckons us both. Remember, "Człowiek nie wielbłąd, pić musi!" (A man is not a camel – he must drink!) One more round, here we go…

Bond on Vodka:
Part 2

"

When [Bond producer] Barbara Broccoli rang me to tell me I'd got the part of Bond, I was buying dishwasher tablets in Whole Foods. I promptly dropped them and went and bought a bottle of vodka!

"

Daniel Craig

I was socking the bottle like crazy. I had maybe two bottles of vodka a day. I'd saturate myself and pass out. It was to insulate me from the madness around Bond.

George Lazenby

I don't think I've drunk one since I've left the Bond movies. Every bar you go in, there's always some wisecrack, 'Oh, yours will be a Martini, shaken, not stirred!' You get sick and tired of that.

Timothy Dalton

I choose vodka.
And Chaka Khan.

Bridget Jones's Diary, *2001*

66

Fifteen bottles of vodka? Yeah, that should do it.

99

The U.S. Office, *"Christmas Party"*, 2005

Crystal Head Vodka is perhaps the most original vodka in the world.

Owned by *Ghostbusters* writer, Dan Ackroyd, to date the brand has sold more than 50 million bottles since launching in 2008. It is filtered by Herikam diamonds and uses original Wisconsin glacier water found underneath Newfoundland.

It won the Gold Medal for Excellent Taste at the 2013 PRODEXPO exhibition in Moscow – beating 400 Russian vodkas!

66

We'd better have
some tea and buns.
Soak up the vodka.

99

The Death of Stalin, *2017*

"

You know, vodka
is for Russians
what therapy is for
Americans.

"

Six Feet Under, *"In Place of Anger"*, 2002

I'll take a cranberry-grapefruit vodka. I know it's called a Sea Breeze. Don't make me say it.

Deadpool 2, *2018*

An old Russian tradition saw
peppercorns dropped
in vodka to soak up any of
the vodka's impurity.

James Bond is seen doing this
in *Dr No* (1952), the first time
Smirnoff was seen on film.

It looks cool. Just one snag –
it doesn't work.

Bond on Vodka:
Part 3

Brands of vodka that have appeared in the
Bond blockbusters:

Thunderball – Smirnoff Blue
Octopussy – Smirnoff Blue
Goldeneye – Smirnoff Black
Tomorrow Never Dies – Smirnoff Red
The World Is Not Enough – Smirnoff Black.
Casino Royale – Smirnoff Red
Quantum of Solace – Smirnoff Black
You Only Live Twice – Stolichnaya
A View To A Kill – Stolichnaya
The Living Daylights – Stolichnaya
Licence To Kill – Stolichnaya
Skyfall – Grey Goose
Dr No – Smirnoff
Die Another Day – Finlandia
Spectre – Belvedere
No Time to Die – Smirnoff Red

Vodka From Around the World

Take your tastebuds on a trip around the world with these popular brands. Where shall we go first?

1. Danzka – Denmark

2. Bombora – Australia

3. Beluga Noble – Russia

4. Grey Goose – France

5. Belvedere – Poland

6. Tito's Handmade – USA

7. Reyka – Iceland

8. Absolut – Sweden

9. Chase – England

10. Ogilvy – Scotland

11. Ketel One – Netherlands

12. 42 Below – New Zealand

13. Crystal Head – Canada

14. Blue Diamond – Estonia

15. Zaranoff – Germany

16. Romanov – India

17. Nemiroff – Ukraine

18. Double Cross – Slovakia

19. Moskovskaya – Latvia

20. Bolskaya – Pakistan

It was the arrival of more than three million Russians, between 1917 and 1922 during the October Revolution and Russian Civil War, to America that kickstarted the States' love affair with vodka.

Harvey Wallbanger

Serving Suggestion
- Ice
- 50 ml vodka
- 1 large or 2 small oranges, juiced
- Half a lemon, juiced
- 15 ml Galliano
- 1 cocktail cherry
- 1 orange slice

Make It Right
Shake the ice, vodka, orange and lemon juice together until the shaker feels cold. Add a few ice cubes to a glass, then strain the cocktail. Pour the Galliano over the top. Dunk a cherry and orange slice for good measure.

167

Guns N Roses lead singer Axl Rose's notorious love of vodka ensured a cocktail became named after him.

The Axl Rose cocktail is champagne and cranberry juice drowned with vodka. Fizzy, sweet and strong!

❝
I've been a
vodka gal since the
beginning of time.
❞

Chrissy Teigen

"

I drink the French 76* –
vodka, sugar, lemon juice
topped up with champagne;
it's the best drink ever. Two
of those and you're like, 'Oh,
life is amazing.' It doesn't
taste at all strong – and
then, whoa, whoops-a-daisy!

"

Kate Moss

* A variation of the French 75 – with vodka instead of gin.

66

Clear alcohols
are for rich women
on diets.

99

Ron Swanson, Parks and Recreation

Absolut, the world's leading Swedish vodka, was founded in 1879 by Lars Olsson Smith. Smith sold his vodka just outside the city's limits at a lower price than vodka made and sold by the state.

He wasn't alone. At the time, 175,000 home distilleries were in business, causing considerable strain on the grain required to make food.

In 1917, the Swedish government monopolized the country's alcohol industry.

In 1997, American businessman Sidney Frank created Grey Goose – arguably the most famous of all top-shelf vodkas. He located the business in France for no other reason than he wanted a high-end vodka that American consumers would immediately associate with luxury.

Every bottle and every cork of Grey Goose vodka is washed with Grey Goose vodka before bottling.

The best disinfectant for vodka is vodka!

❝
White Russian,
no ice, no vodka...
hold the Kahlua.
❞

Halle Berry, Catwoman

From 1945 to the
1970s, one-third of all
revenue generated
by the Russian
government came
from the sale of vodka.

The word "vodka"
is derived from
the Russian for
"little water".

For Halloween 2022, the multi-platinum virtual pop-band, Gorillaz (the brainchild of Blur's Damon Albarn and artist Jamie Hewlett) united with Smirnoff to produce a first-of-its-kind branded bottle of Smirnoff 21.

The collab also included four wacky cocktail recipes – the Vodka Murdini, the Smirnoff Brooklyn, the Vodka Eyeball, and the Sayonara Martini – unique recipes custom-made by the band's members to match their cartoonish personalities.

Vodka Murdini

Serving Suggestion
- 50 ml Smirnoff No.21 Vodka
- 15 ml Belsazar Dry Vermouth
- 10 ml Olive brine
- Dash of saline (optional)
- Pickles (to garnish)

Make It Right
Plunge the Smirnoff, vermouth and brine in a cocktail shaker, and shake until cold. Strain twice. Serve with as many pickles as you DARE. It'll make you *feel good*!

Hangover Cure

In the cult classic 1980 film *Cocktail*,
Tom Cruise's bartender-extraordinaire,
Doug, concocts the perfect morning-
after cocktail. He calls it the Red Eye.
Make it yourself, the next time your
eyes are red, and you have trouble
getting out of bed.

Mix a shot of vodka with tomato juice,
a cracked egg…and cold beer…and
your hangover will disappear.

In 2011, the UK's Black Cow Vodka began making the world's first Pure Milk Vodka.

After noticing the whey they produced when separating curd to make their cheese was going to waste, the clever clogs at Black Cow started putting it to good use. "We take that whey and, using a secret distilling process, turn it into the 'world's smoothest vodka'.

So smooth you can drink it till the cows come home!" so they say.

Try it today, whey-hey!

Vodka may be the healthiest spirit, but a 750 ml bottle of vodka still contains more than 1,600 calories, four-fifths of an adult's RDA.

Ethanol is designed to be as pure as possible, without distinctive character, aroma, taste, or colour. So how can different vodkas taste so different? The trick is in the dilution with water.

When water is used to dilute the ethanol it creates ethanol-water hydrates: an alcohol molecule becomes trapped in a cage of water molecules. The purity and source of water used will alter the hydrate concentration, which will result in a vodka's distinctive character.

490.83

The percentage increase in the Google search term "vodka brands" following the Russian invasion of Ukraine. Searches for "Smirnoff vodka", owned by Britain's Diageo, rose by 177.7 per cent. This increase suggests consumers are checking what brands are Russian before buying.

It requires 10 minutes of jogging – or five minutes of sprinting – to burn off the 100 calories gained by one shot of vodka.

The burn's worth the burn!

In March 2022, after Russia invaded Ukraine, the Stoli Group, officially changed the name of their Stolichnaya vodka – one of the world's leading vodka brands – to "Stoli" in the hopes it sounds less Russian.

"We have made the decision to rebrand entirely as the name no longer represents our organization. More than anything, I wish for 'Stoli' to represent peace in Europe and solidarity with Ukraine," said Yuri Shefler, Stoli's founder.

200

The number of small
potatoes required to make
one 750 ml bottle of vodka.

Vodka Playlist: Big Shot Songs

1. "Shot Through the Heart" – Bon Jovi
2. "Hit Me With Your Best Shot" – Pat Benatar
3. "Big Shot" – Billy Joel
4. "Hot Shot"– Jimmy Cliff
5. "Shot Down in Flames" – AC/DC
6. "Shot in the Dark" – Ozzy Osbourne
7. "Shoot Your Shot" – James Brown
8. "One More Shot" – Tom Petty and the Heartbreakers
9. "Cheap Shot" – Suzi Quatro
10. "Shots" – Lil Jon & LMFAO

In 1994, while staying at the White House, Russian President Boris Yeltsin slipped past security guards and was later found – highly intoxicated on vodka – on Pennsylvania Avenue, dressed in just his underpants, trying to hail a taxi and buy a pizza.

Russian cosmonauts on the International Space Station allegedly have "hidden pockets" sewn inside their space suits that allow them to take a sip of vodka.

Potato Juice

Only 3 per cent of the
world's vodka is made
from potatoes. Bathtub
vodka not included.

"

I hope I've made it right. Six to one sounds terribly strong. I've never had Vodka Martinis before.

"

Solitaire to James Bond, Live and Let Die *(the book), 1954.*

* Bond's perfect Vodka Martini recipe from Fleming's books:
six parts vodka to one part vermouth.